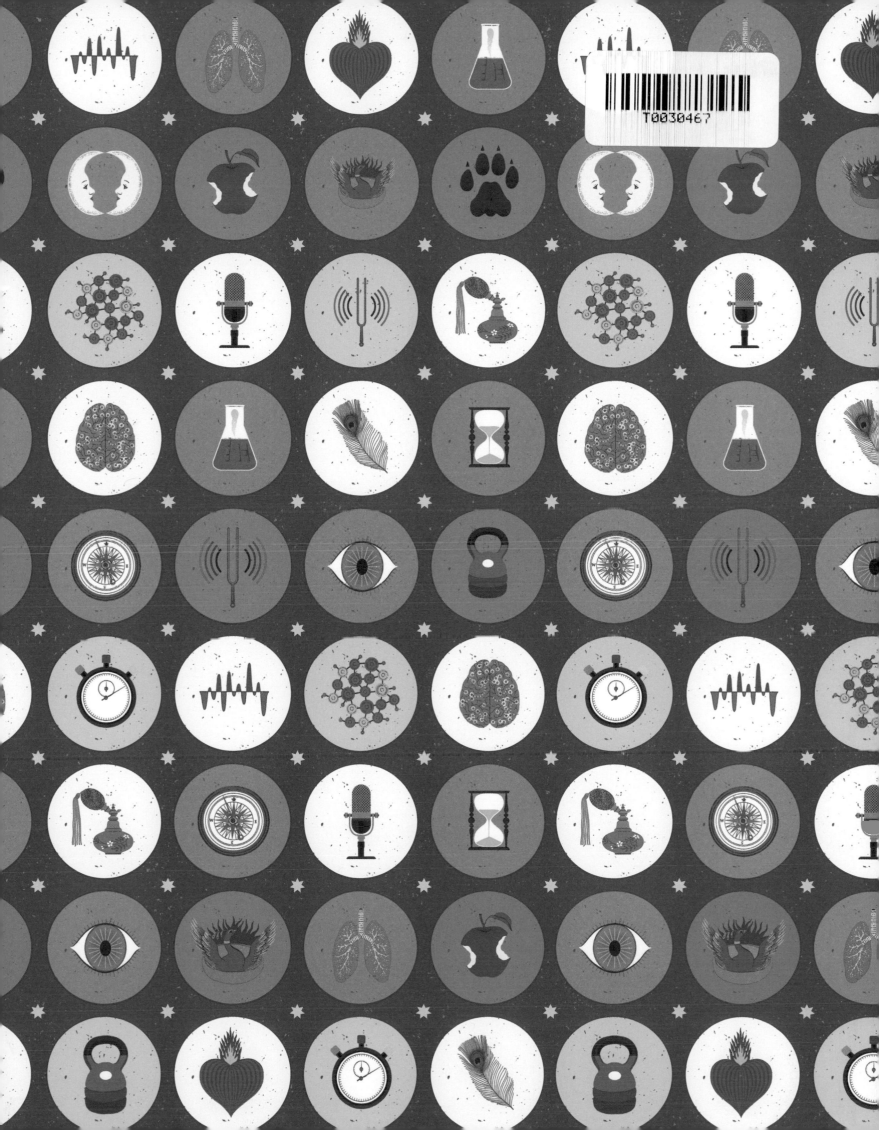

SUPER POWERED ANIMALS

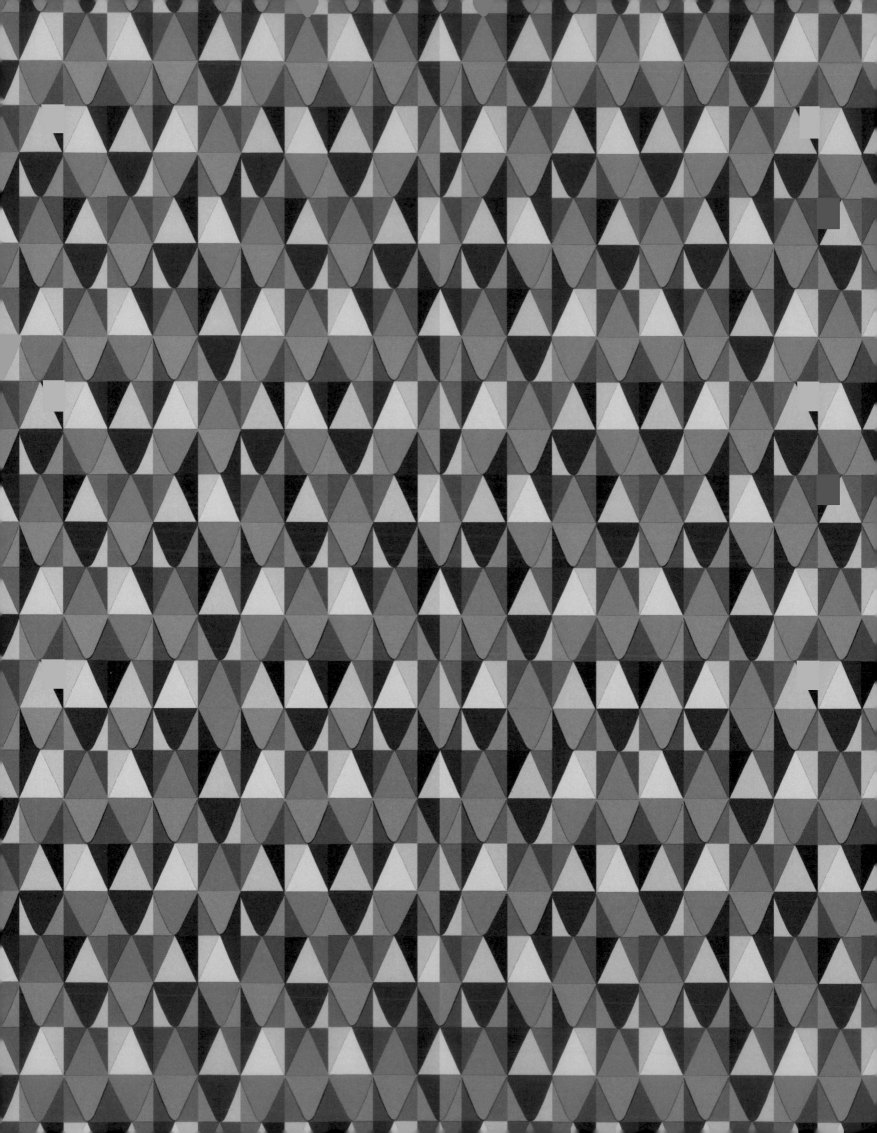

MASTERS
OF
SURVIVAL

For four billion years, nature has been creating forms of life on Earth, from the first bacteria to the most complex animals. Over this long period, certain animals have developed superpowers that make them masters of survival.

These incredible creatures have abilities that far exceed those of humans. They are able to pick up sounds and smells, as well as radio frequencies, electrical impulses, and magnetic fields that we cannot detect. To trick predators or catch prey, they can give off powerful chemicals and even defy the laws of gravity and physics.

This book celebrates these remarkable qualities and presents some of the world's most unique and bizarre creatures.

For example, did you know that dung beetles can pull more than one thousand times their body weight?

Or that polar bears can kill their prey with a single blow from one of their paws?

Or that exploding ants of Malaysia can shoot out a smelly, toxic liquid from their bellies that helps them protect their colony?

Every day, scientists are learning more about these incredible animals to understand how they do the amazing things they do. By understanding how their incredible bodies work, we can better understand the laws of nature. But most important, these fantastic, unique animals can teach us how to take greater care of our planet and all that live on it.

TABLE OF CONTENTS

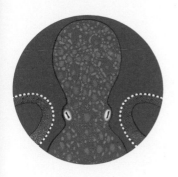

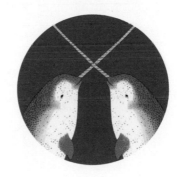

THE SUPERPOWERS

There are species within the animal kingdom that have developed extraordinary survival **skills**. These are some of the **strongest** and **fastest** animals on the planet. Some animals can **regenerate** parts of their body or kill their prey with lethal **venom,** while others have sensational **senses** that would challenge even the mightiest superheroes we can imagine.

SUPER
STRENGTH
Some animals with this superpower have large, muscular, and powerful bodies, while others have incredibly strong exoskeletons (rigid outer skeletons).

SUPER
TOUCH
These animals can detect the slightest vibrations and changes in air pressure, temperature, and wind speed. Sometimes this is through receptors in their skin, antennae, or even hair follicles.

SUPER
SIGHT
Animal eyes can do amazing things with superpowers, such as being able to see in the pitch dark or over long distances. Some animals can even capture images at lightning speed or move each eye independently of the other!

SUPER
CHEMICALS
Many animals use chemicals to defend themselves or attack others. Some use them to attract a mate. Animals might use venoms and numbing chemicals, as well as foul-smelling substances and inks.

SUPER
LEGS
Some animals have limbs that make them move without making a sound or leaving a trace. Some have extraordinary limbs to grip, for climbing, clinging, swinging, or running superfast.

SUPER
SMELL
Powerful smell receptors—usually found on antennae, tongues, or in nasal cavities that are like noses—can tell some animals a lot about their surroundings, the availability of food, and the location of potential mates.

SUPER
HEARING
This superpower helps certain animals pick up sounds over a great distance or even hear ultrasounds (sounds that human ears cannot detect).

SUPER
MIMICRY
Nature's most skilled mimics can change their shape and color, and some can reproduce another animal's sounds and smells. They might camouflage (disguise or hide) themselves or imitate a more threatening predator to scare off an attacker. Some will even play dead.

SUPER BITE

Large, strong jaws with sharp teeth are the weapon of choice for the fiercest predators on the planet.

SUPER VOICE

Certain animals have the ability to make complex vocal sounds. These can warn of danger, express emotions, and might even be made for the fun of it.

SUPER LUNGS

Extraordinary lung capacity allows for some animals to hold their breath for long periods of time underwater. This can help animals, such as polar bears and crocodiles, hunt for longer.

SUPER SPEED

Animals with this superpower are built with bodies that are shaped perfectly to go fast, with exceptional reflexes and agility.

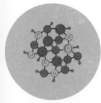

SUPER TEAMWORK

Some species create intelligent communities that must cooperate to survive. Several insect species form giant colonies with millions of individuals. Their shared intelligence and strength, working as one, can be especially powerful.

SUPER SONAR

Echolocation is a kind of super hearing that helps some animals find their bearings, dodge obstacles, and locate prey. An animal sends out sound waves, which bounce off objects and return as an echo, giving important information on the object's size and distance.

SUPER METABOLISM

Some animals have fantastic abilities to slow down their digestion. This helps keep them alive when food is scarce, and conserves the energy it takes to digest food if temperatures are cold.

SUPER REGENERATION

Sometimes animals might lose a body part—for example, a limb or a tail—in a fight. However, certain animals have the amazing ability to grown them back in a process known as regeneration.

SUPER INTELLIGENCE

The animal mind can be superior to the human mind in many ways, especially with memory or the ability to adapt to situations. Some animals are particularly gifted at problem-solving, using advanced hunting and defense strategies and even tools.

SUPER SENSORS

Some species can perceive things happening in our world that we do not have strong enough senses to notice. These can include different colors or sounds, or even smells. This is thanks to their special sensors, which can detect changes in temperature, magnetic fields, ultraviolet rays, and chemical elements in the air.

SUPER CARE

In the animal world, there are several species that adopt orphaned young, spend months building a nest, or who gestate (develop a baby inside their body) and nurse their young for more than a year. For millions of years, these superparents have been making sure of the survival of their species.

Throughout this book, each animal has been awarded a star rating that reflects the number of superpowers it has.

POWERS:

IBERIAN IBEX

The courageous cliff clinger

Daring and agile, the Iberian ibex can scale impossibly steep rock faces and leap skillfully between cliffs. It defies the laws of physics . . . and common sense!

THESE FEARLESS CREATURES ARE KNOWN TO CLIMB TO DIZZYING HEIGHTS OF UP TO 9,800 FEET.

SCIENTIFIC NAME:

CAPRA PYRENAICA

CLASS: Mammalia
ORDER: Artiodactyla
FAMILY: Bovidae

SUPER VOICE

It can make a high whistling sound to warn of danger, as well as a wide range of snorts and noises to express emotions, such as fear or happiness.

SUPER SMELL

The Iberian ibex has a highly developed sense of smell that can warn against predators. A male is even able to detect when a female is ready to mate by smelling her urine.

SUPER TOUCH

Sensitive lips let the Iberian ibex detect changes in temperature, as well as avoid thorny, woody, and grassy stalks while eating.

SUPER LEGS

Its hooves—shaped like suction cups—and strong legs let the Iberian ibex climb nearly vertical surfaces and bare rocks, leaping more than 10 feet between cliffs with ease.

This plant-eating animal helps control the vegetation in alpine meadows and on mountainsides. By grazing and treading on dry vegetation, they can even prevent wildfires from spreading.

SIZE
Males are 4 feet 3 inches to 4 feet 7 inches long (not counting their tail) and weigh 75 to 175 pounds. Male horns can grow up to an astonishing 2½ feet.

COLOR
Their thick, coarse coat is brownish-orange color in summer, turning grayish-brown color in winter.

SPECIAL FEATURES
It has a strong body, with horns shaped like curved swords. Males are bigger than females, and they have larger and stronger horns to fight rivals for the role of dominant male.

LIFE SPAN
Some ibex in captivity have lived as long as 30 years, but most will live between 15 to 18 years.

HABITAT
Mountainous areas of Spain and Portugal where there is tree and grass cover.

DIET
Shrubs and thorn bushes typical of dry and mountainous areas. It also eats tree bark, along with berries, small branches, and grass.

REPRODUCTION
After 5 months, females give birth to one to two kids. From their first day, these young ibex can walk and leap over the cliffs with their mothers.

ENEMIES
Wolves, bears, lynxes, and golden eagles. Humans are also an enemy, because they cause habitat loss and poach Iberian ibex for their prized horns.

POWERS:
✦✦✦
✦✦
✦

AFRICAN ELEPHANT

The giant of the savanna

With incredible strength and highly developed senses, the world's largest land mammal has no equals.

SCIENTIFIC NAME:
LOXODONTA AFRICANA

CLASS: Mammalia
ORDER: Proboscidea
FAMILY: Elephantidae

IT ONLY SLEEPS 2 TO 4 HOURS A DAY, USUALLY ON ITS FEET!

SUPER SMELL ✦

With the best sense of smell in the animal kingdom, it can detect smells over extremely long distances.

SUPER HEARING ✦ ✦✦

With their huge ears and finely tuned hearing, African elephants can hear many sounds that humans cannot.

SUPER TOUCH ✦✦✦

African elephants might be able to "seismically communicate" with other elephants by sensing ground vibrations and low-frequency sounds that humans can't hear. Using sensitive nerve endings in their trunks and feet, they can detect the "sound," or vibration, of distant animals and even pinpoint their location.

SUPER INTELLIGENCE ✦✦✦✦✦

The African elephant's behavior and intelligence can seem similar to a human's. It feels empathy, experiences grief, adopts orphans, uses tools, and is able to recognize itself. What's more, its remarkable memory allows for it to store experiences and knowledge that it remembers when making decisions.

SUPER STRENGTH ✦✦✦✦✦✦

An African elephant can carry up to 10 tons, and its trunk (with thousands of pairs of muscle portions) can lift up to 660 pounds.

SUPER TEAMWORK ✦✦✦✦✦✦

From the time they are born, females live with the same herd of about 15 elephants, led by the oldest one. They form strong emotional ties and show great affection for other herd members. Males live with the herd until they are 12 years old, before forming their own groups.

The African elephant scatters the seeds of many tree species across the savanna through its droppings. Many of these seeds need to pass through its digestive tract before they can germinate.

SIZE
It can grow to more than 10 feet tall and weigh as much as 6½ tons.

COLOR
Its thick skin ranges in color from light to dark gray.

SPECIAL FEATURES
It can use its long trunk to smell, eat, drink, communicate, wash itself, and even handle objects. Large tusks help it forage for food and strip tree bark, as well as to dig for water in a drought. Huge outer ears regulate its body temperature so that it can withstand intense heat.

LIFE SPAN
Between 50 and 70 years.

HABITAT
Warm regions close to sources of water across southern and eastern Africa.

DIET
Grass, leaves, shrubs, fruit, and the bark of trees. It spends most of its time eating and can devour up to 330 pounds of food a day.

REPRODUCTION
When ready, a female elephant bellows loudly to announce her willingness to mate. Several males may fight to earn the right to mate with her. Pregnancy lasts for 22 months and females nurse their young for 2 to 3 years.

ENEMIES
African elephants struggle to see small and fast-moving creatures, such as wasps and rats, and so are fearful of them.

COMMON OCTOPUS

POWERS:

SCIENTIFIC NAME:
OCTOPUS VULGARIS

CLASS: Cephalopoda
ORDER: Octopoda
FAMILY: Octopodidae

LOSING AN ARM IS NO PROBLEM FOR AN OCTOPUS: IT SIMPLY GROWS BACK!

The camouflage artist

In a matter of seconds, an octopus can transform its appearance to protect against predators.

SUPER
MIMICRY

Thanks to pigment-containing cells and muscles, this octopus can change color, shape, and behavior, allowing for it to blend into the seabed or imitate other animals.

SUPER
CHEMICALS

To distract attackers, some octopuses can shoot a jet of thick, dark ink. All octopus species are venomous, but only the venom of the blue-ringed octopus is deadly to humans.

SUPER
REGENERATION

When escaping danger, an octopus can detach one of its arms. The detached arm distracts predators by continuing to wiggle around. The missing limb will later grow back.

SUPER
INTELLIGENCE

The octopus is the world's most intelligent invertebrate (animal without a backbone or internal skeleton). Much like humans, it feels curiosity, and it uses its brain to problem solve and remember information.

SUPER
SIGHT

The octopus has only one type of photoreceptor cell in its retina (an area at the back of the eye) that cannot capture color. However, its U-shape pupils bring in the light in a unique way, from many angles. This possibly lets them "see" color, but in a different way than we do.

Scientists are interested in octopuses not only for their incredible ability to camouflage themselves and regrow lost arms, but also due to their advanced nervous system and impressive intelligence.

SIZE
Although there are giant octopus species, the common octopus normally grows to only about 3 feet in length and weighs about 20 pounds.

COLOR
Usually yellow, brown, and red. However, it can change its appearance by activating special cells found under the skin, known as chromatophores and photophores.

SPECIAL FEATURES
An octopus has eight strong tentacled arms with extremely sensitive suckers on their undersides. These arms come out directly from its head and mantle (body) area, which houses its advanced brain, U-shape eyes, and three hearts, as well as all its internal organs and a beak it uses to eat. A muscular tube, or siphon, next to the octopus's head helps it to move by expelling water like a jet spray, sometimes at great speeds.

LIFE SPAN
Between 12 and 18 months.

HABITAT
Rocky seabeds and caves (which provide good hiding places) in the Mediterranean Sea and eastern Atlantic Ocean.

DIET
The common octopus is a carnivore, eating mainly crustaceans (prawns and shrimp), mollusks (sea snails and clams), fish, squid, and other octopuses.

REPRODUCTION
After the male octopus deposits his sperm into the female's body cavity, the female lays clusters of eggs in a hidden place that is easy to defend. For 4 months, she spends all her time guarding the eggs, without eating anything. When the eggs hatch, the exhausted mother octopus dies.

ENEMIES
Predators include humans, sharks, killer whales, seals, walruses, sea lions, sea gulls, and albatrosses.

SUPERB LYREBIRD

The star performer

Shhh . . . Silence, please. The show is about to start!
The male lyrebird spreads its ornate tail and delights females
with its song. They are mesmerized by this lavish courtship display.

POWERS:

SCIENTIFIC NAME:
MENURA NOVAEHOLLANDIAE

CLASS: Aves
ORDER: Passeriformes
FAMILY: Menuridae

IT CAN MIMIC MANY SOUNDS, INCLUDING NEW SOUNDS SUCH AS CHAINSAWS AND CAMERAS CLICKING.

SUPER VOICE

The male superb lyrebird has some of the most surprising vocal skills in the animal kingdom. It can perfectly mimic any sounds it hears, such as the song of other birds, and even human crying, horns, car engines, gunfire, and alarms. It puts all these sounds and songs together into a "show" that it rehearses all year long so that its courtship ritual will be a success.

SUPER CARE

For several months, the female lyrebird gathers materials for an elaborate nest measuring about 2 feet in diameter, which she maks soft by lining the inside with ferns, roots, and feathers. The male plays no part in in building the nest and does not help incubate (sit on the egg) and raise its chick at all.

SUPER MIMICRY

When performing its courtship ritual, the male lyrebird makes a clearing and dances on a mound of soil it has made into a stage, shaking its magnificent outspread tail and imitating all the different sounds it's gathered over the year. If the female seems bored by its courting performance, it makes the sound of a whole flock of worried birds, to make the female think there is a predator nearby and not want to leave.

As it looks for food, the superb lyrebird scratches the forest floor, helping the leaf litter break down more quickly. This raises the nutrient levels in the soil as well as clears it, making it more difficult for forest fires to spread.

SIZE
About 3 feet long, including its 1-foot 8-inch tail.

COLOR
Its upper body plumage is brown, and the rest of its body is gray, while its tail feathers are brown, gray, and white.

SPECIAL FEATURES
This is a large bird with long and powerful legs that allow for it to run. The male boasts a spectacular and elegant tail, with 16 symmetrical feathers that look like lace. Its two outer feathers are brown and curved. With short, rounded wings, it cannot fly well, so it lives on the ground and sleeps in trees.

HABITAT
The forests of southeastern Australia and Tasmania.

LIFE SPAN
About 20 years.

DIET
Its prey includes earthworms, fleas, cicadas, beetles, larvae, spiders, millipedes, centipedes, ants, wood lice, and scorpions.

REPRODUCTION
After the impressive courtship display, the lyrebirds mate and the female lays a single egg, which she will tend to by herself.

ENEMIES
Large birds of prey, such as the goshawk, as well as foxes, feral dogs, and cats.

TRUE OWL

The lord of the night

In the dark of night, the owl uses its excellent vision and silent wings to swoop down, grasping unsuspecting prey in its lethal talons.

MOST OWL SPECIES CHOOSE A SINGLE MATE FOR THEIR ENTIRE LIFE.

SCIENTIFIC NAME:
STRIGIFORMES ORDER

CLASS: Aves
ORDER: Strigiformes
FAMILY: Strigidae

SUPER HEARING

To locate prey, an owl uses its ears like radar disks, trapping sounds in its "horns," which are the movable tufts around its ears. In some owls, their ears are also set at different heights, meaning there is a time difference between when the sound is picked up by one ear and the other. The owl uses this difference to pinpoint exactly where prey might be hiding.

SUPER SIGHT

To see so well at night, an owl has especially large eyes, with extremely light-sensitive cells called rods in its eyeballs. A super-reflective layer at the back of its eyeball bounces even the tiniest amount of light toward those rods, helping it see in what appears to be complete darkness. An owl, however, cannot move its eye within its socket like a human can do. Instead, to look around, it must use its 14 cervical vertebrae, or neck bones (seven more than humans), to help twist its neck in every direction, including nearly a complete rotation (270 degrees) behind itself.

SUPER LEGS

Owl talons are powerful enough to break a person's arm. The owl is one of the fiercest nocturnal hunters in the animal kingdom.

SUPER SPEED

Its wide wings and exceptional reflexes allow for it to fly at high speed. What's more, the serrated edges of its feathers are designed so it can fly without making any sound and surprise its prey.

Owls keep the population of rodents and insects in check, particularly by hunting mice, which is why they are considered a natural form of pest control.

SIZE
One of the smallest species of owls is the pygmy owl. It measures 6 to 7 inches long and weighs about 2¼ ounces. One of the largest, the Eurasian eagle owl, has a wingspan of up to 6 feet 8 inches and weighs up to 9 pounds.

COLOR
Owls vary in color from brown to snowy white.

SPECIAL FEATURES
A powerful body and wings that are silent in flight. Its large, round eyes are set into the front of its flat face (not on the sides like other birds).

LIFE SPAN
About 5–12 years in the wild and 30 years in captivity.

HABITAT
Owls are found all over the world. They tend to spend their whole lives in the same forest.

DIET
Small and medium-sized mammals (such as squirrels, rabbits, mice), reptiles (lizards), small invertebrate animals (including worms, snails, beetles, spiders), birds (for example, hummingbirds, sparrows), and sometimes fish. Instead of chewing its prey, it tears it into pieces and swallows it whole. After digesting the nutrients it needs, it regurgitates a ball of the inedible parts, such as bones, feathers, and teeth.

REPRODUCTION
The female owl lays between 3 and 11 eggs. When the chicks hatch, the female feeds them with the food brought back by the male.

ENEMIES
Reptiles (snakes), carnivorous mammals (such as foxes, raccoons, cats), and other birds of prey (eagles, falcons, crows, and even larger owls).

CROCODILE

The sensational snapper

Say hi to the reptile with the world's most lethal bite! This fearsome predator is able to hunt both on land and in water.

POWERS:

SCIENTIFIC NAME:
CROCODYLIDAE FAMILY

CLASS: Reptilia
ORDER: Crocodilia
FAMILY: Crocodylidae

CROCODILES EXISTED AS EARLY AS 240 MILLION YEARS AGO DURING THE MESOZOIC ERA, WHEN DINOSAURS WERE ALIVE.

SUPER METABOLISM

Crocodiles can control the speed of their digestion. When food is plentiful and the temperature is warm, it digests its food quickly. However, when food is scarce or the weather is cold, its digestion slows down to conserve vital energy until the next meal, which might be a few months away.

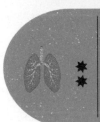

SUPER LUNGS

The crocodile is able to hold its breath for longer than any other animal. It can spend more than one hour underwater without coming up for air.

SUPER REGENERATION

If a crocodile loses any of its extremely sharp teeth it can grow them back. It can grow up to 3,000 teeth over its lifetime!

SUPER BITE

With a bite more powerful than any other animal, the crocodile drags its prey underwater until it drowns, clamps it between its jaws, and spins in a "death roll" until its prey is torn to pieces.

SUPER TOUCH

The small, spotted bumps on a crocodile's skin have nerve endings that can pick up small changes in pressure and vibrations in its surroundings. This is how it locates its prey. The bumps also allow for crocodiles to swim underwater without making ripples.

The crocodile helps to preserve ecosystems by adding nutrients to the water through its droppings. By splashing in the mud, it creates refuges for aquatic animals and plants.

SIZE
Saltwater crocodiles (largest species) reach up to 20 feet and can be over 1 ton in weight. Dwarf crocodiles (smallest species) reach about 5 feet and can be 40 to 100 pounds in weight.

COLOR
Dark green to gray, with hard and scaly skin.

SPECIAL FEATURES
The crocodile is an excellent swimmer. It uses its strong tail—which accounts for almost half its length—to steer and propel its long, flat body in the water. Its back is covered by bony plates with ridges, called keels. Its weakest point is its belly. It uses its four short but strong legs to leave the water, walk, and run.

LIFE SPAN
Between 50 and 80 years.

HABITAT
Swamps, lakes, and slow-flowing rivers of the tropical regions of Africa, Asia, the Americas, and Australia. The saltwater crocodile often lives in estuaries and swims out to sea.

DIET
Fish, reptiles, birds, and mammals of all sizes, as well as small invertebrates, such as mollusks, crustaceans, insects, and frogs. It has no favorite prey and can attack any animal it comes across.

REPRODUCTION
The male crocodile fights to remove any rivals from its territory. Mating takes place in the water. The female will then lay between 40 and 90 eggs in a nest she has made close to the water, which she buries and guards. The babies make squeaking noises when they hatch to alert their mother to dig them out. She then carries them to the water in her mouth.

ENEMIES
Some of the world's most powerful animals, including the lion, leopard, python, hippopotamus, tiger, and elephant. Also human poachers who kill crocodiles for their skin.

COMMON DOLPHIN

The aquatic acrobat

This joyful entertainer can be found leaping and pirouetting through the waves, singing and playing in groups.

SCIENTIFIC NAME:
DELPHINUS DELPHIS

CLASS: Mammalia
ORDER: Cetacea
FAMILY: Delphinidae

MALE DOLPHINS SOMETIMES SERENADE THE FEMALE DOLPHINS TO WOO THEM.

SUPER SONAR ★
The dolphin makes high and low frequency sounds (clicks) that bounce off objects, providing information about the surrounding area. This exceptional system, called echolocation, helps it find its way and locate prey, even at a distance of 300 feet or under the sandy seabed.

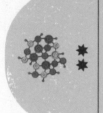

SUPER TEAMWORK ★ ★
Living and traveling in groups, called pods, of about 30 dolphins (but sometimes as many as several hundred), they have strong and lasting relationships with their companions. If one is in danger, another will whistle for help, and the others always respond. Pods will greet each other when they meet.

SUPER INTELLIGENCE ★ ★ ★
Aside from humans, the dolphin is the most intelligent animal on our planet. It is especially known for its incredible ability to communicate and socialize.

SUPER CARE ★ ★ ★ ★
A female will sing to the fetus in her womb with a special whistle during her pregnancy. When the calf is born, this sound will help it to identify its mother.

SUPER VOICE ★ ★ ★ ★ ★
Besides using sound to find its way, the dolphin has a wide range of calls that lets it warn others of danger as well as communicate emotional states.

By hunting fish and squid, dolphins control their populations. This helps to maintain the delicate balance between different species in their ecosystem.

SIZE
Between 6 feet 8 inches and 10 feet long and weighs between 150 and 250 pounds.

COLOR
Gray with a lighter shade on its belly and a darker shade on its back. It often has bands and spots of other shades and colors.

SPECIAL FEATURES
It has a slender and streamlined body and beak, which helps it glide through the water easily. To breathe, its large head has a blowhole on top like a whale. Its tail fin operates like a boat's motor, propelling it through the water, while its pectoral fins, known as flippers, help it to steer.

LIFE SPAN
Between 25 and 30 years in the wild, and as long as 60 years in captivity.

HABITAT
Throughout the world's oceans and seas.

DIET
During its first months of life, it lives on its mother's milk. It will later feed on small fish, squid, crabs, octopuses, prawns and shrimp, as well as other small animals.

REPRODUCTION
Mating is a quick process, but it is repeated several times a day between different males and females. After 11 months, the female gives birth to a single calf. Because the father's identity is unknown, all the males in the group will look after all the calves. Mothers nurse their young for up to 2 years.

ENEMIES
The largest dolphin species have no predators. The smallest ones are threatened only by killer whales and some shark species, as well as by humans.

COMMON VAMPIRE BAT

The blood guzzler

With razor-sharp teeth and the ability to numb its victims before feasting on their blood, you can see why the vampire bat got its name.

SCIENTIFIC NAME:
DESMODUS ROTUNDUS

CLASS: Mammalia
ORDER: Chiroptera
FAMILY: Phyllostomidae

THE BAT IS THE ONLY MAMMAL THAT CAN FLY.

SUPER HEARING
★

It detects the low and constant breathing noise made by its prey (mainly cows) as they sleep deeply, taking advantage of this to attack.

SUPER CHEMICALS
★★
★★

A common vampire bat's saliva contains an anesthetic that numbs its victims and an anticoagulant that stops blood from clotting. This enables it to drink blood for 30 minutes without its victim noticing.

SUPER TOUCH
★
★★
★★

A bat has rows of tiny hairs on its wings that work like sensors that enable it to detect and react instantly to the slightest changes in wind direction and speed. They help it to control its flight and make sudden turns and dives.

SUPER SONAR
★★
★★
★★
★★

The common vampire bat makes high-pitched sounds (inaudible to human ears) that bounce off objects and give information on the surrounding area. This echolocation helps it fly in total darkness without colliding.

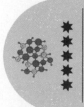

SUPER TEAMWORK
★★
★★
★★
★★
★★

It lives in large colonies and shares its food with families that have been unable to feed (a bat will die if it goes more than two nights without feeding). It is able to regurgitate the blood it has drunk and give it to its companions.

SUPER SENSORS
★
★★
★★
★★
★★
★★

Temperature sensors in its nose help find warm-blooded prey and locate the part of its victim's body with the greatest blood flow. It doesn't actually suck the blood—it laps it up with its tongue.

This bat pollinates flowers that bloom at night. There are about 500 types of flowering plants in the world that depend on bats for pollination, as an essential part of their reproduction process.

SIZE
Between 2½ and 3½ inches long and weighs about 1½ ounces.

COLOR
Shades of brown and gray.

SPECIAL FEATURES
Its body is covered with a coat of short hair that protects it from moisture and cold. Unlike other types of bats, it uses its strong back legs to walk, run, and jump.

LIFE SPAN
Between 12 and 35 years.

HABITAT
Caves in tropical regions of Mexico and other Central American and South American countries. It sleeps in total darkness, hanging upside down from the ceiling.

DIET
The common vampire bat is a carnivore and hunts at night. It needs to drink ¾ ounce of blood (half its body weight) per day—that's about 4 teaspoons daily.

REPRODUCTION
Males and females mate with different individuals within the same colony, reproducing throughout the year. After a pregnancy lasting 7 months, between two and four babies (known as pups), are born completely developed. The female nurses its pups with milk. Males care for and protect all the pups in their colony.

ENEMIES
This bat can be attacked by owls during its nightly outings.

PEREGRINE FALCON

SCIENTIFIC NAME:
FALCO PEREGRINUS

CLASS: Aves
ORDER: Falconiformes
FAMILY: Falconidae

The sky racer

When the majestic peregrine falcon flies, the rest of the world seems to move in slow motion.

MALE FALCONS PERFORM SPECTACULAR AERIAL ACROBATICS TO COURT FEMALE FALCONS.

SUPER SPEED

The peregrine falcon is the world's fastest animal. Its powerful V-shape aerodynamic body is designed to cut through air at high speed and perform precision maneuvers midflight. Nothing can rival its famous dive, which sees it plunge at speeds of more than 186 miles per hour. Naturally, this skill makes it a merciless hunter. Flying horizontally in short pursuits, it can reach a speed of 75 miles per hour. Aeronautical engineers have studied its physical features to design more streamlined aircraft.

SUPER SIGHT

This bird's eyesight is almost three times better than that of humans. This is because its eyes are more tubular in shape, with large pupils containing a huge number of photoreceptor cells to see more detail. Its excellent sight is combined with an ability to quickly process what it is seeing. Because its eyes are particularly large compared to its head, it is difficult for it to move its eyes in different directions. Unless it is directly in its line of vision, a peregrine falcon has to turn its head to study faraway prey.

As the fastest and most lethal bird, it maintains the balance in its ecosystem by eating and keeping down the populations of other birds. Airports use peregrine falcons, because their presence scares away other birds, preventing them from flying over runways and crossing flight paths.

SIZE
It is a medium-size bird that grows 13½ to 23 inches long, with a wingspan of 4 feet (the male is smaller). It weighs between 1 pound 10 ounces and 3 pounds 5 ounces.

COLOR
Dark blue-gray feathers on the top of its body and wings, with white throat and undersides, both speckled with black. Black feathers on the nape and front of the head resemble a helmet.

SPECIAL FEATURES
A rounded head with a hooked beak. It has short legs with especially strong talons. Its wings are narrow and pointed.

LIFE SPAN
Between 12 and 15 years. However, six out of every ten falcons do not survive their first year of life.

HABITAT
In mountainous regions, and on hills and coastal cliffs of every continent except Antarctica. It is also found in woods within some urban areas.

DIET
A carnivore, it mostly feeds on the birds it hunts in flight. On rare occasions, it has been known to catch bats, rats, mice, hares, and squirrels.

REPRODUCTION
It mates once a year and always in the same place. The female lays between two and five eggs, which it sits on for about 30 days. Once hatched, young falcons make their first flight after 40 days.

ENEMIES
Owls are known to attack a nest, to feed on a falcon's eggs and chicks during the day, and on unwary adults at night.

GRASS SNAKE

The greatest actor

Never trust this trickster. It may appear dead but don't get too close . . .

POWERS:

SCIENTIFIC NAME:
NATRIX NATRIX

CLASS: Reptilia
ORDER: Squamata
FAMILY: Colubridae

SUPER MIMICRY

Because it isn't venomous, the inoffensive grass snake has developed a creative defense strategy—playing dead to ward off predators. This animal behavior is known as thanatosis. During its display, it remains motionless on its back with its belly swollen with air, imitating the bloating caused by gases when a body is decomposing.

SUPER CHEMICALS

Another of its "playing dead" abilities is to leave its mouth open with its tongue hanging out (with a few drops of blood), while rolling its eyes. As a final flourish, it expels a foul-smelling liquid with its droppings in hopes of repelling any hungry predator.

SUPER SMELL

Like all snakes, the grass snake uses its tongue to smell. By sticking it out and flicking it around, it can detect chemical substances in the air to help it track its prey or hide from nearby predators. It can also help to find a mate or identify other grass snakes to share its shelter when hibernating.

With plenty of predators and its own large appetite for amphibians and fish, this semiaquatic snake plays an important role in the food chain within wetland ecosystems.

SIZE
Females can grow to a length of 4 feet, while males rarely exceed about 3 feet.

COLOR
Usually olive green, although grass snakes can also be gray, bluish, and black. They have small black markings and a lighter colored belly. Grass snakes are also known as ringed snakes, because of the collar—a partial ring of white or yellow edged with black—seen on the necks of younger snakes. This collar fades as the snake gets older.

SPECIAL FEATURES
A long and flexible body covered in scales with a pointed tail and a rounded head. Unlike other snakes, it has round pupils, it lays eggs, and it can stay underwater for up to an hour.

LIFE SPAN
Between 15 and 25 years.

HABITAT
Waterside woodlands, wetlands, and drier ecosystems near rivers or other bodies of water, across much of Europe as well as North Africa and western Asia.

DIET
Mainly frogs and toads, although it also feeds on mice, fish, lizards, insects, and earthworms.

REPRODUCTION
After mating, the female looks for a sheltered place that is warm and moist (rotting vegetation or manure), where it lays 10 to 40 eggs. When they hatch, the young snakes are the size of a pencil and completely independent.

ENEMIES
Birds of prey (eagles, owls, hawks, and buzzards), large wading birds (herons and storks), and mammals (martens, badgers, genets, otters, hedgehogs, and cats).

GREAT WHITE SHARK

The sharp-sensed swimmer

INSIDE THE WOMB, THE STRONGEST SHARK FETUSES EAT ANY EMPTY EGGS.

Special electricity sensors in the shark's skin allow for it to detect any living creature moving in the water. Now that's a superpower! And if its prey decides to hide on the seabed? Bad idea . . .

SCIENTIFIC NAME:
CARCHARODON CARCHARIAS

CLASS: Chondrichthyes
ORDER: Lamniformes
FAMILY: Lamnidae

SUPER SENSORS

A network of tiny openings in the shark's head lead to jelly-filled channels that are sensitive to electric fields. These receptors, known as ampullae of Lorenzini, pick up the electric signals left by moving prey—even under the seabed. These sensors can detect Earth's electromagnetic field, working like a compass to show the way on long journeys.

SUPER SIGHT

Its eyes have a membrane, or thin layer, that reflects and magnifies even the smallest amount of incoming light in deep, dark waters. Its highly developed eyesight is crucial when closing in on its prey.

SUPER SMELL

Water enters into the great white shark's olfactory bulb—its organ for smelling—through two nasal cavities, or nares, in its head. This organ can "smell" a blood molecule in among a million other water molecules, helping it track its prey.

SUPER BITE

A great white shark bite is 300 times stronger than a human's. To be sure of its deadly effect, its mouth is equipped with several rows of large, serrated, and razor-sharp teeth.

This shark cleans the seabed of dead animals. It eats old and diseased fish, balancing their communities and preventing the spread of disease.

SIZE
A great white shark is between 12 and 20 feet long (it never actually stops growing) and can weigh between 1 and 2 tons. The female is larger than the male.

COLOR
Despite its name, only the underside of this shark is white; the rest is a bluish-gray color. This camouflages it against the dark seabed, when seen from above, and helps it to look like the sun's rays when seen from below.

SPECIAL FEATURES
A strong body with two large pectoral fins and the unmistakable triangle-shape dorsal fin. Its tail fin, known as the caudal fin, is shaped like a crescent. It has a conical snout, with a huge, rounded mouth. It has five gill slits on each side of its body, and its skin is covered in hard, toothlike scales.

LIFE SPAN
More than 70 years.

HABITAT
Relatively shallow waters of warm and temperate oceans and seas. It lives close to rock or sandy shores, where it finds the most food.

DIET
Fish, dolphins, sea lions, squid, octopuses, cuttlefish, turtles, penguins, dead and rotting animals, birds, and even other sharks.

REPRODUCTION
The male transfers his sperm to the female to fertilize her eggs. A year later, the eggs hatch inside the female's womb and she gives birth to baby sharks, known as pups. Three or four pups hatch at a time, and they immediately swim away from their mother to avoid being eaten.

ENEMIES
This shark's only natural predator is the killer whale, although its main threat is from humans.

EXPLODING ANT

POWERS:

SCIENTIFIC NAME:

COLOBOPSIS SAUNDERSI

CLASS: Insecta
ORDER: Hymenoptera
FAMILY: Formicidae

The deadly detonator

This ant is small but courageous. When under attack, a worker ant won't hesitate to burst open its stomach and spray a toxic liquid at its enemy, sacrificing itself to protect its colony.

SUPER CHEMICALS

Female worker ants of this species store a sticky and toxic substance inside their abdomen that can burn and immobilize their enemies. But to use this poison, they have to burst open their stomach, killing themselves in the process.

SUPER TEAMWORK

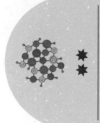

The exploding ant lives and works for its colony, made of millions of individuals that collaborate as one to make sure of the survival of all. Their superpower is the ability to work together.

SUPER SMELL

Ants have the most smell receptors of any type of insect on the planet (more than 400, compared to the 60–80 of most insects). If one of these ants explodes, the released chemicals can be "smelled" in the air, alerting the rest of the colony to protect the nest.

SUPER STRENGTH

Ants can carry up to 50 times their own weight using their small but powerful jaws.

About half of all herbaceous plants on our planet depend on ants to scatter their seeds. In return, ants receive a protected place, where they can build their nest and obtain food.

SIZE
Between ¼ and ½ inch long.

COLOR
Dark brown, red, and black.

SPECIAL FEATURES
Two antennae on its head that are bent like an elbow. It has a small jaw. Its abdomen, which is much larger than that of other ants, produces and stores the corrosive substance.

LIFE SPAN
Worker ants of this species live for 2 years and the queen lives for 15 years.

HABITAT
Tropical rain forests of Malaysia and other parts of Southeast Asia.

DIET
The exploding ant is an omnivore (it eats everything). It feeds on dead insects, fruit, flowers, flesh, and fat.

REPRODUCTION
The queen ant mates with a number of different male ants, known as drones, which die soon after mating with her. The queen lays hundreds of eggs every day for the rest of her life. Female worker ants tend to the eggs during their delicate growth cycle. Larvae destined to become queens are fed a higher-quality diet.

ENEMIES
Frogs, toads, lizards, snakes, spiders, and birds.

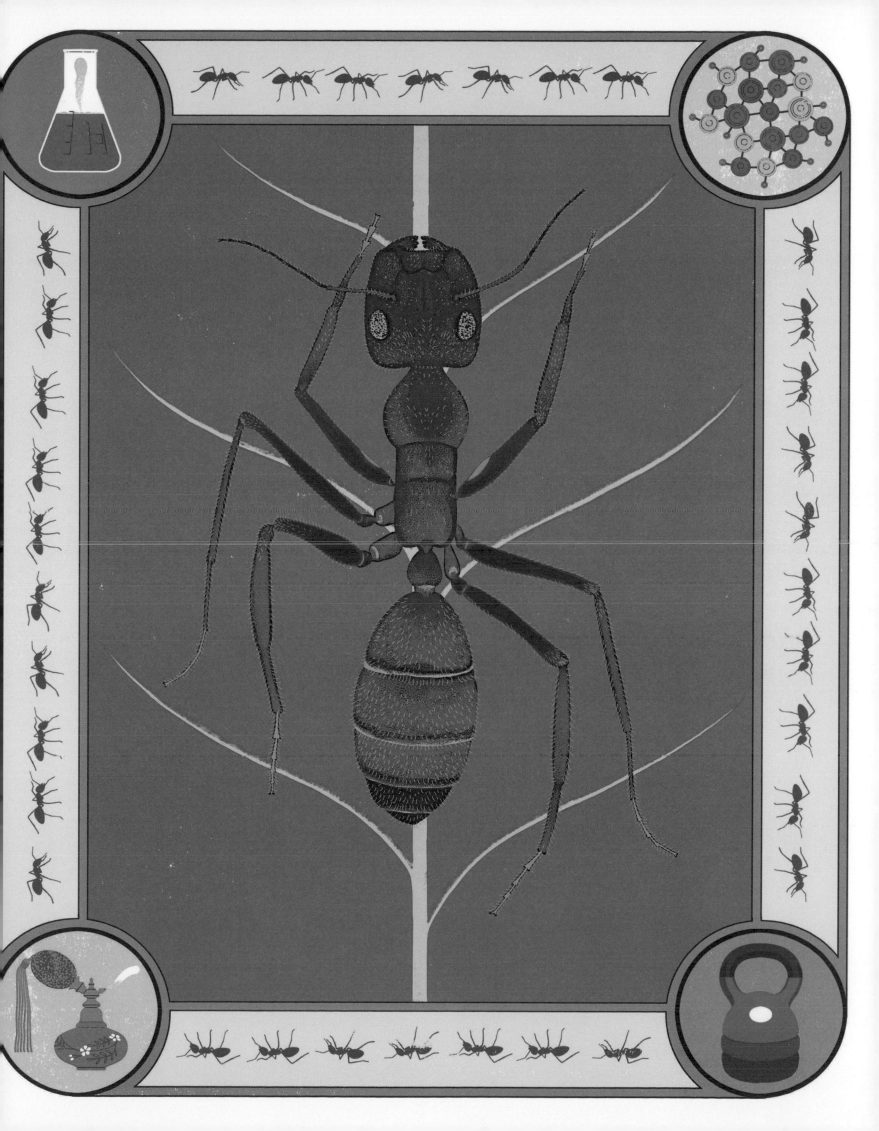

MOTH

The mysterious mimic

The moth is an expert at mimicry. The amazing patterns on its wings perfectly mimic animals that pose a threat to it.

POWERS:

★ ★ ★
★ ☆ ★
★ ★

SCIENTIFIC NAME:

SATURNIIDAE

CLASS: Insecta
ORDER: Lepidoptera
FAMILY: Tineidae

AFTER TRANSFORMING FROM A CATERPILLAR, SOME MOTHS STOP EATING AND ONLY REPRODUCE.

SUPER
SENSORS

Thanks in part to tiny hairs on its antennae, a moth can detect pheromones, a chemical substance, from other moths up to 5 miles away. These chemicals help moths communicate with each other about food, existing dangers, and mating.

SUPER
SMELL

The moth's smell receptors are located in its antennae. Hawk moths can "smell" the particular chemical signature of the flowers they like with their antennaae and their tongue.

SUPER
HEARING

The moth has the sharpest sense of hearing of all animals. Some species can hear ultrasound waves of up to 300 kilohertz, which are inaudible to humans. These are the same frequencies used by bats, which helps the moth avoid hunting bats.

SUPER
MIMICRY

The moth is a master of camouflage. The patterns on its wings imitate those found in its environment, or on the insects that pose the most danger to it, such as wasps and spiders, or they might resemble the shape of bird droppings. Camouflage provides protection from its most lethal predators.

Plants that bloom at night largely depend on moths to pollinate them. There are 250,000 moth species, and they are found all over the world.

SIZE
Moths vary greatly in size, ranging in wingspan from less than ¼ inch to nearly 1 foot.

COLOR
The wings have dark eye spots.

SPECIAL FEATURES
The wings, bodies, and legs of moths are covered with dustlike scales that come off if the insect is handled. Compared with butterflies, moths have stouter bodies and duller coloring.

LIFESPAN
The male moth lives for about 30 days, while the female lives half this time, at most.

HABITAT
Highly adapted, it can be found everywhere from high mountaintops to deserts. The moth is a nocturnal creature and is found in dark spaces.

DIET
The larvae and adults of most moth species are plant eaters.

REPRODUCTION
As with all lepidopterans, the moth life cycle has four stages: egg, larva (caterpillar), pupa (chrysalis), and adult (imago).

ENEMIES
Birds, bats, and spiders, among others.

NARWHAL

The unicorn of the sea

With its extraordinary tusk, formed from an extremely long tooth, the narwhal looks like the mythical single-horned creature after which it is nicknamed.

POWERS:

★ ★
★ ☆
★ ★

SCIENTIFIC NAME:
MONODON MONOCEROS

CLASS: Mammalia
ORDER: Cetacea
FAMILY: Monodontidae

ONE OUT OF EVERY 500 MALE NARWHALS HAVE TWO TUSKS.

SUPER TOUCH
★

As well as being used to stun and disorientate fish before they are eaten, the narwhal's "magic" tusk has millions of nerve endings that are sensitive to temperature, salt levels, and water pressure. This information can tell a narwhal the depth at which it is swimming, the location of gaps in the ice where it can breathe, and even when it will snow.

SUPER VOICE
★ ★

The narwhal uses a variety of vocalizations, including whistling, clicking, and buzzing to communicate with other narwhals and locate prey.

SUPER CARE
★ ★ ★

A female narwhal gives birth to only one calf, which she nurses for up to 20 months. In this time they form a very close and special bond. The calf remains within two body lengths of its mother at all times.

SUPER SONAR
★ ★ ★ ★

The narwhal has what is possibly the best echolocation system on the planet. When a sound is released and its sound waves "bounce" back in the form of an echo, some animals can use the echo's information to get a sense of the object's size and location. This is called echolocation. By sending out a series of clicks, a narwhal can get a good "image" of potential prey or obstacles.

Narwhal and whale droppings are usually nutrient-rich and are a source of food for microscopic plants, known as phytoplankton, and tiny crustaceans, known as krill. Many animal species feed on both.

SIZE
About 13 to 16 feet in length and between 1,750 and 3,500 pounds in weight.

COLOR
A narwhal is born with evenly colored blue-gray or blue-black skin. As it grows, its skin lightens while developing a blackish mottled pattern. The skin of old narwhals is practically white.

SPECIAL FEATURES
The adult male narwhal has a tusk that grows in a spiral. It begins as a canine tooth that emerges from the left side of his jaw and protrudes out to a length of up to 10 feet. Females rarely have this tusk.

LIFE SPAN
Between 50 and 70 years. Narwhals don't survive in captivity.

HABITAT
In the winter, the narwhal lives in the icy waters of the North Atlantic Ocean, close to sheets of sea ice. In summer, they migrate to the coastal areas of the Arctic Ocean.

DIET
Mainly consists of fish, but also squid and krill. To catch food, it can dive to depths of about 1 mile for up to 25 minutes.

REPRODUCTION
Narwhals mate in a vertical position, with the male joining its belly to that of the female in order to transfer its sperm. After a pregnancy lasting 15 months, the female gives birth to one calf.

ENEMIES
Sharks, polar bears, and killer whales. However, pollution and climate change are the main threats faced by narwhals today.

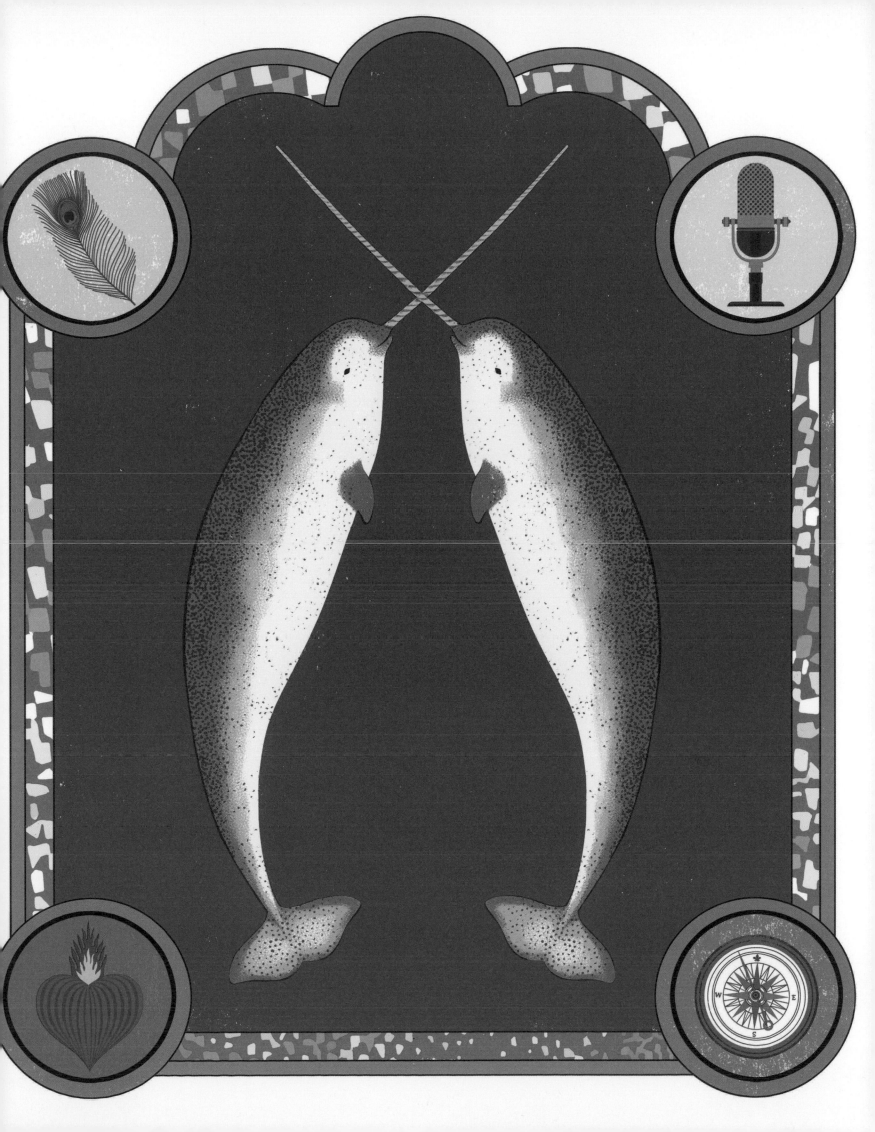

BULL-HEADED DUNG BEETLE

The amazing weight lifter

Surprise! For its size, this tiny dung beetle is the strongest creature in the animal kingdom. Even Superman would be impressed!

POWERS:

SCIENTIFIC NAME:

ONTHOPHAGUS TAURUS

CLASS: Insecta
ORDER: Coleoptera
FAMILY: Scarabaeidae

ONCE A DUNG BEETLE IS FINISHED COLLECTING DUNG INTO A BALL, IT ROLLS IT HOME IN A PERFECTLY STRAIGHT LINE.

SUPER STRENGTH

This beetle, which has an extremely strong exoskeleton, can lift up to 1,141 times its own weight. Its two back legs do almost all the work, rolling the enormous balls of dung it makes.

SUPER SMELL

Dung beetles have sensitive antennae with hundreds of smell detectors that can pick up the smell of animal droppings, their main food source, over a great distance.

SUPER SIGHT

Dung beetles are able to see the light of the Milky Way, and they use the Sun and Moon to find their way. There are no obstacles that will make them change their course, including steep slopes and steps.

It breaks up, scatters, and buries animal droppings, helping to disperse seeds, prevent flies that might carry diseases, and fertilize the soil.

SIZE
Between ¼ and ½ inch in length.

COLOR
Black or reddish tone with a silvery sheen on its back.

SPECIAL FEATURES
A body divided into three parts; head, thorax, and abdomen. Its rounded head has two antennae and two protruding horns that give the beetle its name. Three pairs of strong and hairy legs protrude from its thorax. Its entire body is protected by a strong exoskeleton. On both sides of its abdomen are holes, called spiracles, through which it breathes.

LIFE SPAN
About 1 year.

HABITAT
Every continent except Antarctica. It can adapt well to different habitats. It digs tunnels where it buries the dung balls it makes.

DIET
Dung, which is high in carbohydrate, vitamins, minerals, nitrogen, and bacteria.

REPRODUCTION
The male shapes dung into a large ball into which the female will insert three or four eggs. When the larvae hatch, the dung ball will be their food.

ENEMIES
Insects, reptiles, birds, and mammals.

POLAR BEAR

The Arctic powerhouse

This majestic predator is one of the most feared animals on the shores of the Arctic Ocean. There's no escape from one, either on the ice or in the water.

POWERS:
★★★
★★★
★

SCIENTIFIC NAME:
URSUS MARITIMUS

CLASS: Mammalia
ORDER: Carnivora
FAMILY: Ursidae

WHEN A POLAR BEAR COMES OUT OF THE WATER, ONE SHAKE IS ENOUGH TO DRY ITS BODY.

SUPER SMELL
★
The polar bear probably has the most powerful sense of smell in all the animal kingdom, after the African elephant. It can smell prey or dead animals 18½ miles away. It also uses its highly developed sense of smell to locate and identify other polar bears.

SUPER BITE
★★
The polar bear has 42 very large and sharp teeth. Its bite is more powerful than that of the Bengal tiger and African lion.

SUPER SIGHT
★★★
Its eyes have a third eyelid that acts like sunglasses, filtering the glare from the light reflected on the ice.

SUPER CARE
★★★★
When a female polar bear becomes pregnant, she eats more than she needs to build up her energy reserves. She stays in her den for months to give birth to and suckle her blind, toothless, and totally helpless cubs. She will later teach them how to look for food and protect themselves.

SUPER STRENGTH
★★★★★
It takes only a single blow of its paw for a polar bear to kill its prey and remove its victim effortlessly from the water.

SUPER LUNGS
★★★★★★
Polar bears can hold their breath when 3–5 metres underwater for 2 minutes. They can swim hundreds of kilometres without a rest.

SUPER LEGS
★★★★★★
Each of its paws has five hooked claws to catch prey and walk on snow. Tufts of fur that grow between its paw pads stop them from slipping on the ice. The polar bear is also especially fast, reaching top speeds of 25 miles per hour.

It plays a vital role in keeping the seal population under control. It also feeds on walruses, beluga whales, musk oxen, reindeer and birds and their eggs.

SIZE
An adult male weighs 770 to 1,540 pounds and can grow to more than 8¼ feet long. A female tends to weigh half as much and grows to about 6½ feet.

COLOR
The polar bear's coat is actually translucent—it appears white from the way light is reflecting off its hairs. These hairs are hollow and filled with air, which acts like insulation to keep the heat in. The polar bear has black skin (like its nose) under its coat to absorb and store the sun's heat. And it has a blue tongue!

SPECIAL FEATURES
It has short but strong legs, a flattish head, and especially large and powerful jaws. Its short tail and small ears help reduce heat loss. A thick layer of fat under its skin gives it further protection against the cold.

LIFE SPAN
Between 25 and 30 years.

HABITAT
The Arctic.

DIET
The polar bear is the world's largest land-dwelling predator. This hungry carnivore needs to eat 65 pounds of food each day. It mainly hunts seals to eat their fat and skin. It doesn't drink water, because it obtains all it needs from the blood of its prey.

REPRODUCTION
Females mate only every 3 years (this causes a great deal of fighting between males during the mating season).

ENEMIES
The polar bear has no natural predators. Threats, however, include climate change and humans, who encroach on its habitat and hunt it.

BLACK WIDOW SPIDER

SCIENTIFIC NAME:
LATRODECTUS MACTANS

CLASS: Arachnida
ORDER: Aranaea
FAMILY: Theridiidae

The small and silent terror

Although she is generally peaceful and solitary, the black widow can be deadly. Courting her is a mission filled with danger—she will kill and eat her partner after mating.

THE BLACK WIDOW'S VENOM IS 15 TIMES MORE POWERFUL THAN A RATTLESNAKE'S.

SUPER CHEMICALS

To trap insects and other arachnids, a black widow uses silk fibers produced in her abdomen to make a web that is as tough as steel. Once its prey is caught in the web, the black widow injects it with venom and then covers it with digestive enzymes—chemicals that break it down to make it easy to ingest. A female black widow's venom is very strong but it will only attack in defense—its bite is dangerous to humans but rarely fatal.

SUPER TOUCH

The black widow spider picks up sounds and vibrations from the air through the hairs on its feet. It also detects static electricity in the atmosphere. These abilities help it understand its surroundings, making up for its lack of hearing and poor sight. They can tell it about the presence of potential prey, and through vibrations in the web, the female can communicate with her mate.

Black widows keep insect numbers in check. Scientists are studying the properties of its remarkable web and venom.

SIZE
With their legs completely extended, a female black widow spider can grow to 1⅜ inches, while a male grows to only ¾ inch (it also weighs 30 times less than the female).

COLOR
The female is shiny black with a red hourglass-shaped marking on her abdomen. The male is brown and black, with four pairs of red and white stripes on both sides of his abdomen.

SPECIAL FEATURES
Its body is divided into two parts: a head, which is joined to its thorax (from which its eight long legs emerge), and an abdomen.

LIFE SPAN
Between 1 and 3 years.

HABITAT
The black widow spider likes dark, sheltered holes or openings in objects. It hides amid stones, pieces of wood, and the bark of trees. It is mainly found in the dry regions of the eastern United States and Mexico.

DIET
Insects, such as beetles, flies and mosquitoes, and other arachnid species.

REPRODUCTION
The male weaves a small package that he fills with sperm. He then carries it on one of his legs to the female in order to fertilize her. The female lays her fertilized eggs in bundles, each in a different sac that she hangs on her web. The newly hatched spiders eat their siblings, leaving few survivors.

ENEMIES
Birds, insects, and small mammals.

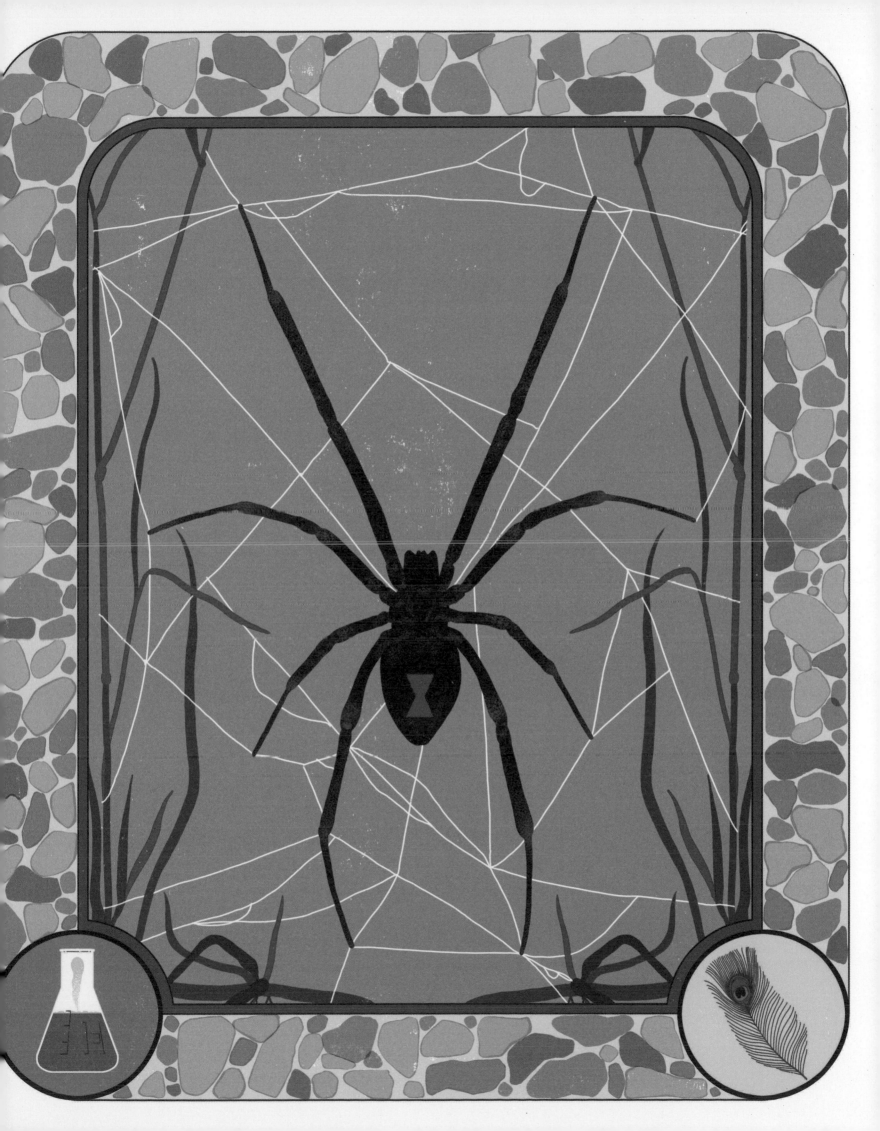

CHEETAH

The super speeder

This incredibly fast big cat can almost defy the laws of nature. Its body is designed to fly with its feet on the ground.

SCIENTIFIC NAME:
ACINONYX JUBATUS

CLASS: Mammalia
ORDER: Carnivora
FAMILY: Felidae

DESPITE BEING A MEMBER OF THE CAT FAMILY, THE CHEETAH CANNOT ROAR OR CLIMB TREES.

SUPER SPEED

This is the world's fastest land animal, with a top speed of 70 miles per hour over distances of 1,300 to 1,600 feet. It can accelerate from 0 to 60 miles per hour in only 3 seconds, and it can change direction at high speed.

SUPER SIGHT

It has high-set eyes, which can take in an extremely wide 210-degree field of view, and specially adapted retinas, the part of the eye that receives light, allowing for it to see far and wide across the flat, open landscapes it tends to live in.

SUPER LEGS

Like all felines, the cheetah is a digitigrade, which means that it walks on its toes. The undersides of its feet are lined with hard pads that keep it from sliding in mud, helping it chase prey over wet ground. While almost all other felines can draw their claws in completely, the cheetah has semi-retractable claws, which helps it to grip and quickly build up speed.

SUPER INTELLIGENCE

Because the cheetah uses up huge amounts of energy when racing at high speed, in order to use its energy efficiently, it uses its exceptional intelligence to predict which way its prey is going to run before springing into action.

SUPER CARE

The mother cheetah lives alone with her cubs until they are adolescents. Female cheetah's have also been known to adopt orphaned cubs.

The cheetah helps to balance its ecosystem. By hunting animals that are underdeveloped, weak, or ill, which are easier to catch, it supports the survival of better adapted individuals.

SIZE
Smaller than most of the big cats, its body is 3 feet 7 inches to 5 feet long, not counting its tail, which is 1 foot 10 inches to 2 feet 8 inches, about half the length of its body. It weighs between 75 and 130 pounds.

COLOR
Tawny with black spots and a white throat. Unlike the leopard, it has black lines that run from its eyes to its mouth. Its spots are also smaller and more rounded.

SPECIAL FEATURES
Its thin body is designed for racing. It has a strong heart (the largest of all felines in proportion to its body), large lungs, and wide nostrils to keep good levels of oxygen and blood circulating through its body while it hunts. Its long tail gives it stability when chasing prey, helping it change direction quickly.

LIFE SPAN
From 10 to 12 years in the wild, and more than 20 years in captivity.

HABITAT
Wide and open expanses of land, such as grasslands and semidesert regions mainly across Africa and western Asia.

DIET
A carnivore, it mainly eats gazelles and impalas, although it sometimes hunts larger mammals, such as wildebeests and zebras.

REPRODUCTION
The cheetah reproduces throughout the year. A female ovulates only after mating with a male. Her pregnancy lasts between 90 and 100 days. She gives birth to three to five cubs. The mother rears her cubs alone, teaching them to hunt after only a few months.

ENEMIES
Larger scavengers, such as the hyena, and other predators, such as the lion and the leopard, which tend to steal the animals killed by the cheetah. For this reason, it tends to hunt in the middle of the day, when its enemies are usually asleep.

PUFFER FISH

The spiky poisoner

Don't be fooled by the comic appearance of this strange-looking fish— its poison can kill up to 30 people.

POWERS:

SCIENTIFIC NAME:
TETRAODONTIDAE FAMILY

CLASS: Actinopterygii
ORDER: Tetraodontiformes
FAMILY: Tetraodontidae

ONLY EXPERIENCED CHEFS KNOW HOW TO PREPARE PUFFER FISH WITHOUT THE RISK OF DEATH FOR THE PERSON EATING IT.

SUPER MIMICRY

If a predator gets too close, this small and harmless-looking fish quickly fills its flexible stomach with water and air. This turns it into a ball and makes its spines stand on end. Some species of puffer fish, which is also known as blowfish, can change color to blend into their surroundings.

SUPER CHEMICALS

Puffer fish spines contain tetrodotoxin, a poison that is 1,200 times more lethal than cyanide. The puffer fish is the world's third most poisonous vertebrate (animals with a backbone). No antidote has yet been found for its deathly toxin.

SUPER SIGHT

This family of fish has excellent sight, which helps them quickly identify any approaching predators. The puffer fish can also look right and left at the same time, because its eyes move independently. This lets it capture every detail of its surroundings.

Its powerful poison can be used to make medicine that relieves patients from pain caused by injuries.

SIZE
This varies greatly depending on the species. The dwarf, or pygmy puffer fish, is only 1 inch long, while the giant puffer fish can reach a length of 2 feet.

COLOR
Typically a greenish-yellow color with black markings that cover its whole body.

SPECIAL FEATURES
The puffer fish has a long and robust body covered with sharp spines. It has a wide, bulky head and big eyes. Its mouth has reinforced lips and four teeth shaped like a beak that it uses to crush its prey. Behind its weirdly cute appearance is an aggressive and temperamental fish.

LIFE SPAN
Between 8 and 10 years.

HABITAT
Most puffer fish species (there are more than 120) live in warm tropical and subtropical waters. They tend to prefer shallow waters close to coral reefs. Some species live in fresh water.

DIET
An omnivore, it eats seaweed and small invertebrates. The larger species can crack shells with its beak and eat clams, mussels, and other sea creatures.

REPRODUCTION
For more than a week, the male puffer fish devotes all its time to creating perfect circles with beautiful geometric shapes on the seabed. This impressive feat attracts a female to lay its eggs inside the circle, which the male then fertilizes.

ENEMIES
Sharks and large fish. Pollution, habitat loss, and overfishing by humans are its main threats.

CAT

The stealthy assassin

Prowling the streets in the early hours of the morning, this light-footed hunter will stalk its prey, preparing to pounce.

SCIENTIFIC NAME:
FELIS SILVESTRIS CATUS

CLASS: Mammalia
ORDER: Carnivora
FAMILY: Felidae

CATS CAN JUMP 5-6 TIMES THEIR HEIGHT. THAT'S LIKE A PERSON JUMPING 3 STORIES!

SUPER SIGHT

The cat can see in near darkness, thanks to a membrane called the *tapetum lucidum* at the back of its eyes, which reflects the little light available. It is what makes their eyes glow at night.

SUPER HEARING

It can detect extremely high pitched rodent sounds that are inaudible to humans. Each ear has 32 muscles and can turn independently of the other to detect the source of the sound. Talk about cutting-edge technology!

SUPER SMELL

The cat's sense of smell is 14 times sharper than that of humans. It uses smell to find food and mates, to identify another cat's territory, and to locate the people they live with.

SUPER TOUCH

Using its whiskers, it can detect changes in air pressure as well as wind speed and direction. Because its whiskers are connected to its nervous system, the slightest vibration will put the cat on alert.

SUPER LEGS

Like all other digitigrade animals, the cat walks on its padded toes, enabling it to detect the temperature of the ground, move silently, and leave little trace of its path.

The cat is a particularly effective hunter. Because it is a domesticated animal, it keeps rats and mice away from the houses it inhabits.

SIZE
About 18 inches long (not counting the tail) and weighs between 4 and 20 pounds.

COLOR
A cat can be black, white, shades of gray, orange, and yellow. A cat with more than three colors is almost always a female. The coat of hair that covers a cat's body can be especially thin (almost invisible), curly, short, medium, semilong, or long.

SPECIAL FEATURES
A cat's body has 230 bones that give it extraordinary flexibility and elasticity. They normally have a tail, although certain breeds are tailless. Its claws are retractable, and they keep them tucked away when not being used to keep them sharp.

LIFE SPAN
Between 12 and 18 years.

HABITAT
All over the world. Together with the dog, the cat is the world's most popular domestic animal.

DIET
The cat is a carnivore and will hunt small rodents and birds, but as a domesticated animal its main diet consists of commercial cat food (which contains rice, corn, and other plants, as well as animal protein).

REPRODUCTION
When the female cat is ready, it stops eating and lets out dramatic wails that announce its willingness to mate. A male cat may have to fight with rivals before mating. After 62 to 67 days, the female will give birth to four to six kittens, which she will care for and nurse diligently.

ENEMIES
Dogs aren't a cat's worst enemy. What it's really afraid of is being surprised. A cat doesn't like loud noises (you only have to see its behavior during a thunderstorm or when fireworks are let off to know this).

IBERIAN WALL LIZARD

The daredevil climber

This agile and stealthy reptile defies gravity to scale vertical surfaces and can even detach its tail to outwit attackers.

SCIENTIFIC NAME:
PODARCIS HISPANICUS

CLASS: Reptilia
ORDER: Squamata
FAMILY: Lacertidae

LIZARDS BASK IN THE SUN TO RAISE THEIR BODY TEMPERATURE.

SUPER LEGS
The soles of this lizard's feet have pads with thousands of microscopic hairs that "stick" to flat surfaces. Combined with the lightness of its body, these pads help it cling to vertical or even upside-down surfaces.

SUPER REGENERATION
When threatened, this lizard squeezes certain muscles to make its tail drop off. This distracts the enemy, allowing for the lizard to escape. Special cells in its stump help to regrow the tail.

SUPER SMELL
Thanks to its sharp and sensitive tongue, even a newly hatched lizard can distinguish the smells of other lizards from those of predators. A lizard will sometimes use scent marks to decide on a mate before seeing it.

SUPER SIGHT
Many lizards have a third eye, called the parietal eye, that sits at the top of their head. Small and usually covered by skin, it cannot see in the same way as its other two eyes. Instead, it detects sunlight and even acts as a kind of compass to help with navigation.

SUPER INTELLIGENCE
A male lizard has a unique strategy to communicate and defend its territory. This consists of a series of head nods, tail twitches, and foot shakes.

It effectively controls plagues of snails, locusts, and other insects that threaten crops. In urban areas, it keeps down the number of mosquitoes, flies, spiders, beetles, and worms.

SIZE
Between 1½ and 2¾ inches from the tip of its head to the base of its tail. Its tail can measure 4 inches, sometimes double the rest of its body. Females weigh no more than ⅛ ounce. The male is a little larger.

COLOR
Skin color and patterns can differ, but typically it is a dark green color (sometimes with a reddish back, neck, and head). Its belly is lighter.

SPECIAL FEATURES
It has a flat head, slender body, and long tail. Its body is covered by thick and impermeable skin and small scales. It has four legs, each with five pads.

LIFE SPAN
About 10 years.

HABITAT
Rocky regions across the Iberian Peninsula (Spain, Portugal, and Andorra), as well as northern Africa and northeast of the Pyrenees mountains in France and Spain. It finds shelter between rocks and in tree trunks, cracks in walls, and other nooks and crannies.

DIET
Different types of insects, including ants, flies, and mosquitoes, as well as wood lice and spiders.

REPRODUCTION
When a female is ready to mate, males hold races and fights to earn them the right to mate. The female lays several batches of two or three eggs and hides them. When the baby lizards hatch, they eat the same things as their mother. At 2 years old, they are ready to mate.

ENEMIES
Larger lizards, snakes, small mammals (such as weasels and genets), and birds (owls, kestrels, and red kites, among others).

HONEYBEE

SCIENTIFIC NAME:

APIS MELLIFERA

CLASS: Insecta
ORDER: Hymenoptera
FAMILY: Apidae

The great pollinator

This little insect houses state-of-the-art technology inside its body and plays a vital, supersize role in the creation of food and household items on which humans depend.

THE HONEYBEE CANNOT SEE THE COLOR RED.

SUPER CHEMICALS
★

The queen bee gives off pheromones, a mix of chemicals that, once picked up by other bees' antennae, helps control all the beehive's activities. The queen and worker bees can also use a venom to defend themselves by jabbing their stinger into an attacker. Unlike worker bees, the queen doesn't die when she uses it.

SUPER INTELLIGENCE
★★

The bee performs a unique dance, called a waggle dance, to indicate to other bees where there is food. The type of dance that is performed is related to the distance to the food. The exact distance and direction is marked by the number and speed of the turns it makes.

SUPER SENSORS
★★★

Hairs covering a bee's body detect the electric fields of flowers, allowing for the bee to return to the same flower and know whether another bee has already visited. A magnetic mineral (known as magnetite) acts like a compass inside a bee's abdomen, helping it to navigate while it flies.

SUPER TEAMWORK
★★★★

A bee colony is a superorganism arranged in three distinct groups: the queen, worker bees, and drones. Worker bees, the most numerous, are tasked with the upkeep of the hive and colony.

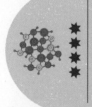

SUPER SIGHT
★★★★★

Bee eyes can perceive ultraviolet light, invisible to human eyes, and can clearly distinguish the edges of flowers.

SUPER CARE
★★★★★★

The bee colony is a matriarchy. Ruled by the queen, she keeps it united and lays the eggs.

An essential plant pollinator, the honeybee also makes royal jelly to feed its young, honey to provide worker bees with energy, and wax to build honeycombs.

SIZE
It is ½ inch long.

COLOR
Brown with a black and yellow-striped abdomen and dark brown legs.

SPECIAL FEATURES
The queen bee, the only fertile female, has a large and prominent abdomen equipped with a stinger. The worker bee, a sterile female, has a pollen basket on her back legs, as well as a stinger. The drone, or male bee, has a larger head and thorax than the worker. It has a bullet-shape abdomen without a stinger.

LIFE SPAN
The queen bee lives for 3 years. A drone can live for 3 months, while a worker bee lives for 2 to 7 months, depending on the amount of work to be done in the hive.

HABITAT
Europe, North Africa, and a part of Asia, wherever flowers grow. In the wild, it lives in a hive built in trees, usually under branches or in hollows that form in the trunk.

DIET
Pollen (worker bees), honey (drones, worker bees), royal jelly (newly hatched worker bees and the only food eaten by the queen).

REPRODUCTION
A number of drones will mate with the queen in flight. The drones die after mating, while the queen will lay 1,500 eggs each day in hexagonal cells inside the hive. Each new larva that hatches from an egg is fed by young worker bees, known as nursing bees. After 1 week, the larva is sealed into its cell, and an adult bee will emerge about a week later. Larvae hatched from fertilized eggs will develop into worker bees, while those hatched from unfertilized eggs will develop into drones.

ENEMIES
The wasp and small hive beetle are major enemies.

Phaidon Press Inc.
65 Bleecker Street
New York, NY 10012

phaidon.com

This edition © 2023 Phaidon Press Limited
First published in Catalan as *Superpoders animals* in 2023 by Zahorí Books
Sicília, 358 1-A · 08025 Barcelona
www.zahoribooks.com

Text © Soledad Romero Mariño 2023
Illustrations © Sonia Pulido 2023

ISBN 978 1 83866 722 1 (US edition)

006-0723

A CIP catalog record for this book is available from the Library of Congress.

Printed in China

Scientific editing: Martí Badal
Design and layout: Joana Casals
Editing: Miguel Vándor

Commissioning Editor: Maya Gartner
Project Editor: Alice-May Bermingham
Production Controller: Rebecca Price
Translated by Cillero & de Motta

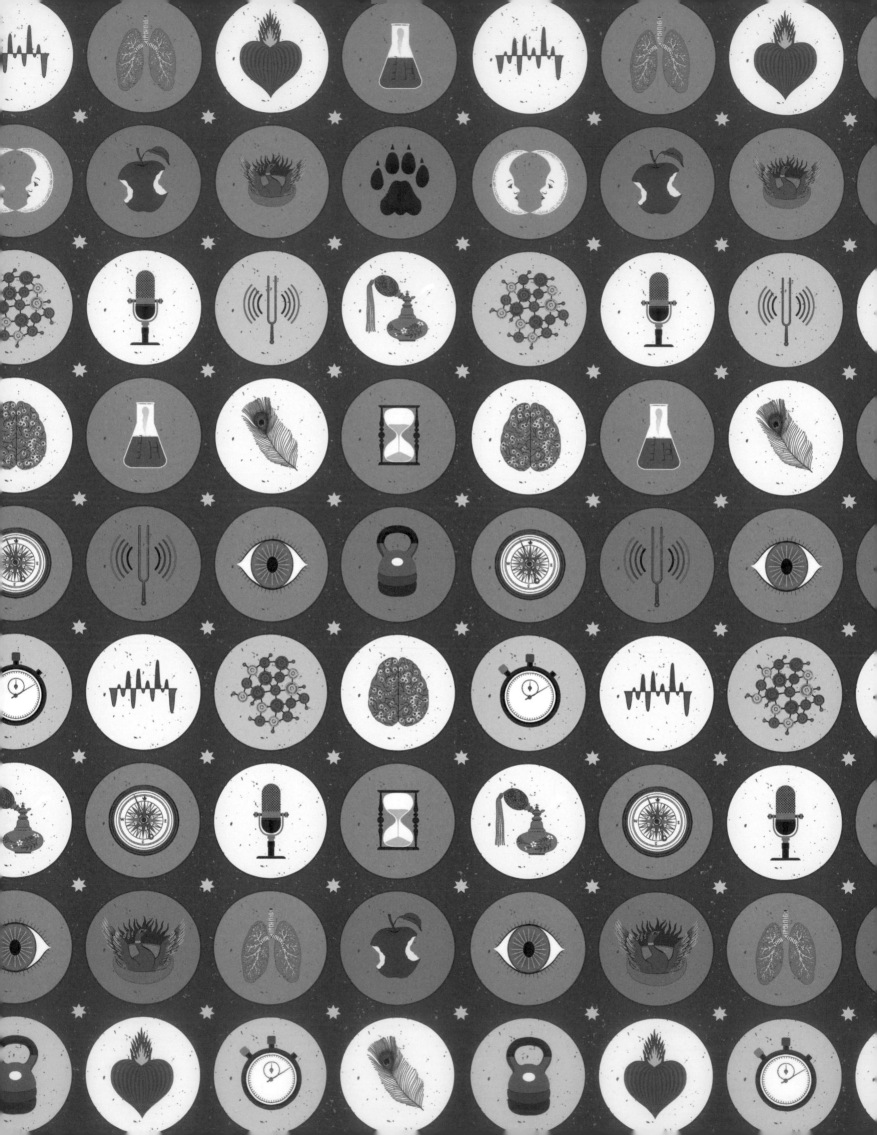